THE

SELF

DIRECTING

PROFESSIONAL

By Derek Biddle & Ali Stewart

NOW PIONEERING
PROFESSIONAL.

PDG Books Ltd

ISBN 978-1-905519-08-8

Cover design and artwork by PDG Books Ltd

Printed by ASK Print Ltd

Also by Derek Biddle, PhD, MSc, CPsychol, AFBPsS, FIPB;
Leading & Developing High Performance

From the book's Foreword by Ali Stewart:-

"Leading & Developing High Performance helps leaders to lead with strength and dignity, passion and compassion. It gives leaders a track to run on, taking them on a sure path from transactional to transformational leadership.

This book captures the essence of what high performing leaders do to create sustained high performance.

The book is supported by a full training programme and set of diagnostic tools, which help strengthen leadership capability within organisations. Ali Stewart & Co is the accrediting body for any trainers wishing to be accredited to deliver the programme - www.alistewartandco.com "

ISBN 978-1-905519-05-7

Contents Page

Introduction

What makes high fliers fly?

How is it that some people become very successful very quickly, they get promoted earlier than most and at the same time they seem to have a very good life outside work?

Why is it that other people who work very hard struggle to achieve the same success?

How do you lift yourself up and demonstrate the kind of personal excellence that the really effective people display?

We set about researching this in a major UK organisation, and became very excited by the results. Then we carried on researching in many other organisations. The findings were the same. Our research demonstrated that what differentiated the successful, effective people from others who were less effective, was one **Key Attitude** and a **Set of 7 Skills**.

The effective people had naturally acquired this mindset and skills, and it was nothing to do with having a high IQ. It was more to do with EQ - **Emotional Intelligence**, taking charge of your own learning and life, being **Self Directing**. The exciting part is that these skills can be studied and learnt by anyone.

This is supported by all the recent champions and authors of self development like Daniel Goleman (author, 'Emotional Intelligence'),

'The good news is that emotional intelligence can be learned. Individually we can add these skills to our tool kit for survival at a time when 'job security' seems like a quaint oxymoron.'
Daniel Goleman

'... having these capabilities offers each of us a way to survive with our humanity and sanity intact, no matter where we work. And as the work changes, these human capacities can help us not just to compete, but also nurture the capacity for pleasure, even joy, in our work.'
Daniel Goleman

and even the not so recent authors...

'... fifteen percent of your earning potential comes from knowledge and direct skills, the other eighty five percent comes from leadership and interpersonal skills.'
Dale Carnegie

So, understanding and practising the attitude and skills of the **Self Directing Professional** is key to developing your own personal excellence. We would like to lead you through a process for doing just this; it is a journey we invite you to come on with us.

Through this 'pocket guide' you can refer to a process for doing just this. You can learn what makes the high flyers fly; and acknowledge and brush up the fine skills you already possess.

Are you ready? We will start with a stock take of how you are doing right now.

Derek Biddle & Ali Stewart

Chapter 1: The Self Directing Professional

Are You A Work Victim?

Consider the following situation:

Julian had looked forward to his new job and to a successful career with this organisation. He had anticipated steady promotion and a lifetime of satisfying, interesting and responsible work using the expertise he had worked so hard to gain. But it is not like that at all.

It is not that there isn't plenty to do; he feels he is chasing his tail most of the time and can never get on top of things. He takes instructions diligently but often finds that he's embarked on a frustratingly wrong course of action once he's got the task. His manager seems very busy, and doesn't devote enough time to Julian's development and career. Encouragement and attention are in short supply, although people are friendly enough.

Julian feels he could do more demanding work, but he doesn't really know how to, anyway he might make mistakes or increase his workload. He did take on a project once but tripped over some of the political nuances rife in the organisation and the project wasn't a real success. Often he feels he has to work in the dark and guess at what is required of him, only to be hit by totally unexpected problems. Moreover everything seems to change all the time, as soon as he grasps a situation somehow it moves on to something different.

He has had some contact directly with clients, but they seem not to want to hear about his depth of knowledge and elegant solutions, but simply to get their own needs satisfied. Although it might cost more, Julian feels frustrated that such people can't see and appreciate what is on offer.

In the end he loses heart; his enthusiasm has waned although out of necessity he still puts in long hours. He feels stressed and powerless and has little energy outside work to do the things he thought he wanted to do. He marks time waiting for an opportunity to arise where life could be better. Meanwhile there is yet another organisational change due. He will see what fate has in store for him.

Julian has become a **work victim**. It is not a good place to be. It may be comfortable in the sense that the responsibility is seen by him to lie elsewhere, and he cannot do very much about it except reduce his expectations and settle for a 'quiet' life. However, it is not a very secure, satisfying or rewarding place to be. Rather it has its own stresses, frustrations and dissatisfactions. No-one gains, most of all Julian.

Complete the following quick self assessment to see where you are on the **work victim** scale. The totals at the end of each column will tell their own story, it needs little interpretation!

Are you a **Work Victim**? If you <u>Strongly Agree</u> or <u>Agree</u> with a good number of the following questions you may well be on the way to becoming one	Strongly Agree	Agree	Disgree	Strongly Disagree
1 I have little control over the way my work is done				
2 I get little satisfaction from the work I do				
3 The people who get in the way of me achieving real success are my managers				
4 I feel stressed most of the time I am at work				
5 My contribution is not well recognised				
6 There is little opportunity to learn new skills around here				
7 No-one takes any interest in my career				
8 Things were much better in the 'old' days				
9 I feel frustrated and powerless				
10 I do not really know what I want to do in the future				
11 I do not know how to achieve my aims				
12 I feel that others less able than me succeed faster				
13 I am not in control of what happens to me				
14 The demands made on me are impossible				
15 I am bored, under-stretched and under-utilised				
16 I am always having to fight the system or my manager				
17 I am not appreciated properly				
18 I do not really know what is expected of me				
19 My strengths are not recognised and used				
20 Other employers provide much better opportunities				
Total number of responses for each column	A	B	C	D

How can I create my own success and excellence?

It is not by waiting for ...

the perfect manager There isn't one. Many are good, most busy, but it is highly unlikely that any will be as interested in your success and career as you are.

the perfect organisation Again, there isn't one. Some clearly are better than others, but the 'grass is greener' syndrome is often a trap.

the perfect environment Same news again, some better than others, but none perfect.

the perfect job Some people spend a lifetime hoping to come across this. They rarely do.

It is like waiting for the *perfect world*, it has not happened yet, at least not over the last 4000 years. It may happen some time into the next 4000. Are you prepared to wait, or would you rather make the best use of what is available NOW?

This brings us to the **Key Attitude** that distinguished the people who succeeded in work and life. They took **responsibility** for **creating their own success** through **managing their own environment**. They were **Self Directing**. Instead of seeing themselves as passive victims of their environment, having everything done unto them like this:

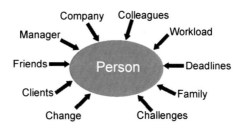

...their view was more one of shaping their own environment, like this:

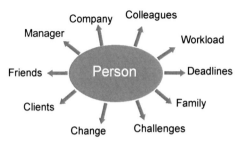

So Whose Business Is It Anyway?

Self Directing people see themselves as managing their own business. Their business is themselves. For those in employment, like the majority of us, they operate a **business** within a business. They realise that no-one cares as much about their own success as themselves and that operating this way has a win:win outcome for everyone.

Most of us work for a living, unless we were born with the proverbial "silver spoon", have a rich aunt or win the lottery! These days our security comes from our employability, the value added skills we have to offer in the marketplace. One aspect of **Self Directing** behaviour is to keep such skills current. If you do not invest in your own business how can you expect other people to do so?

Operating a **business within a business** puts a perspective on your life at work and on taking responsibility for yourself to achieve what you want. At one level this may be security, as described. At another it may be promotion, or money, also achieved from a platform of being excellent at what you do. For many people it is the satisfaction and achievement of excellently doing interesting, useful work.

As well as this your **business** is not just the work part of it, but life overall. Do you want to manage this part of your business so you really get what you want, to have excellent outside work as well as within, or perhaps to strike the right balance between the two? The principles and skills of **Self Direction** will be of great value in life generally. That is the added bonus.

Our Development as People

When you start to understand and embrace the **Key Attitude** of highly successful people, it is useful to look at the way people develop generally. There are also reasons why there is sometimes a dissonance between the way people behave inside work compared with their life outside.

As a baby or child we are, of course, entirely **Dependent** on others to feed, clothe and nurture us. Part of growing away from this state can result in teenage rebellion or **Counter-Dependency** where we test our own boundaries and discount what others have told us. This (with any luck!) is followed by early adulthood where we have evolved a sense of who we are and what matters to us. We also feel competent to deal with most of life and function OK with it, although our main preoccupation is still ourselves. We see ourselves as **Independent** people, responsible to ourselves.

The next significant stage is into maturity, where we are no longer just **Independent**, making our own informed decisions and coping well, but where we have the capability to operate at another level, co-operating well with other people from the security of our own platform of self worth, capable of taking their needs into account and proactively managing our own environment. This is true **Interdependency**; we make choices rather than being driven by events or conditioning.

This four stage process is described on the next page.

8

Dependency	Directed, nurtured and sustained by others
Counter-Dependency	Rebelliousness, taking irresponsible initiative, being preoccupied with self
Independency	Taking care of self, becoming inner-directed and self-reliant, thinking own thoughts, making own decisions
Interdependency	Being self-reliant, proactive and capable, but also being able to join with and share productively the resources of other people

Not all people make this journey to its full extent of course. Some get stuck permanently in **Dependency**, either by choice or as a coping adaptation, some, few, are permanently rebelling, others are self-sufficient Independents who do not make the next step embracing the potential richness of others.

Often, as mentioned, there is a dissonance between behaviour inside work and that outside of it. Frequently this is because of expectations, the expectation that one will be told exactly what to do and be directed, that the manager is there to take care of all needs, and anyway they are paid to do so - a view often reinforced by managers under the *Command and Control* system that some still use. So people get habituated to this - if that is what they want that is what they will get - and 'jobs-worth' enters the scene. Other people see themselves as pursuing meaningless, boring jobs and do not invest themselves psychologically in them. Others, by default and design find their fulfilment outside work. What happens too frequently these days is that people are suddenly required to operate in an **Interdependent**, empowered fashion overnight. This is scary and a not uncommon response is to stay with what is familiar, particularly if you are not sure the organisation really means what it says.

These are just some of the reasons which sometimes inhibit people from operating to their full abilities. They may or may not apply to you but, once the choices are made clear, most people elect to strive towards the way of life of **Interdependence**.

The Self Directing Professional

Let's now identify more closely the **Key Attitude** and resulting behaviours of the highly effective people we have described. We will start by getting out of the way what they are NOT!

Firstly, they are not **Dependent** 'subordinates':
• **Dependent** people take on a strongly subordinate role. They take all their problems to their manager, and expect their manager to solve them. They would not even think about trying to solve the problem for themselves. Rather they like being told what to do. They depend on others to manage them, their work and their needs.

They are relatively powerless people who tend to blame others and the situation for any difficulties they encounter. They are not self starters and often see themselves as 'victims' of a situation. Their manager is likely to see them as weak and ineffectual.

And they are not **Counter Dependent** 'subordinates':
• Over Independent or **Counter Dependent** people also take on a subordinate role. They see a problem, decide that this is a chance to prove themselves by doing things their own way, and fail to keep their manager or colleagues appropriately informed. They ignore the wider view and are dismissive of others' inputs; solutions are often not good quality ones.

In the manager's eyes the **Counter Dependent** subordinate resists control, thinks that they know it all, seeks personal glory and does not appreciate the manager's needs. Because of their over independence, managers do not trust them and supervise them closely to head off trouble. They show lots of initiative - too much in fact - but little sense of real responsibility.

We have called both these two types of behaviour 'subordinate' behaviour because they put their manager in a situation of having to supervise them closely.

But neither are they **Independent**:
• **Independent** people tend to be good corporate citizens. They try and do what is right in a responsible way. They are engaged with their work and focus on their tasks, but they often feel swamped by their workload and it is sometimes difficult to get their head above the horizon. They could take on more interesting, challenging work but find getting the balance right quite difficult.

Such people often identify strongly with the technical issues they deal with and prize their expertise. They are skilled and clear in presenting problems to their managers. They tend to be obliging and courteous and help others when asked to do so. Sometimes they wonder why their conscientiousness is not better recognised, for example they notice that other people tend to make a greater impact and are promoted earlier. Often they feel they are taken for granted. Although they put in effort and are willing to relate to other people, and put in a good performance, this performance seldom achieves an 'excellent' level. Their life outside work is OK, but sometimes they wonder whether they could make more of the opportunities life has to offer.

They **ARE Interdependent Self Directing people**:
• **Self Directing** people see a problem and take responsibility for ensuring it is dealt with. They present solutions not problems. They take responsibility for creating their own success, managing their own environment and working with others in a proactive and genuine way. In dealing with situations they take the broad view, asking themselves 'If this was my company, what would I do?' which necessarily includes taking the needs of everyone into account.

What are the crucial key differences between these four ways of operating? They are to do with initiative and taking responsibility for doing so, in a way which we describe as …

RESPONSIBLE INITIATIVE

For example:
- **Dependent people**…
do not use initiative, they rely passively on other people's, and neither do they accept responsibility for themselves

- **Counter Dependent** people…
seize initiative but use it irresponsibly, regardless of other people and the wider implications

- **Independent people**…
use initiative but in a limited way within self imposed boundaries, restricting their own capability. They are respectful of responsibility, accept it, but often take a limited view towards it including for proactively managing their own situation. Most people tend to operate in this way, both at work and in their lives generally.

- **INTERDEPENDENT**, **Self Directing people**…
take personal responsibility for creating their own success and managing their own environment, using **Responsible Initiative** to do so.

Having a **Self Directing** orientation based on **Responsible Initiative** is the single most important difference in being in control of one's own life and success, and which differentiates the effective people who achieve excellence, from the less effective.

Responsible Initiative is the **Key Attitude**. Of course this attitude has to be backed up by some key skills which we will look at next, but what matters is having this key approach, ability and mindset to put it into practise.

The Seven Key Skills of Self Directing People

So what are these key skills which are so important and which, when aligned with the approach of taking **Responsible Initiative**, have such an effect both in work and in everyday life? They are a generic set, many of which are concerned with interacting with people, the people being you as well as others:

A **Self Directing person**;

1. **Clarifies what is to be done**
Questioning and listening to explore what is required of them, to reduce ambiguity and explore expectations; to establish a clear brief.

2. **Has strategic business awareness**
Can think strategically, as well as tactically and operationally in the context of business; shows common sense and has a solid understanding of commercial issues.

3. **Controls own workload/manages projects effectively**
Has the practical skills of delivering successfully to meet differing requirements, including political ones; manages own workload well.

4. **Negotiates for success**
Is able to negotiate positively to get best possible results, particularly when there are conflicting priorities and needs, and to achieve **win:win** outcomes.

5. **Manages relationships/knows own strengths**
Understands individual differences well, including customers, colleagues and manager; makes best use of own and others' strengths; deals with conflict constructively.

6. **Manages own learning**

Has fundamental skill of managing own development and continuous improvement in constantly changing environment; self-reliant; acquires self-directed learning skills to create continuous learning; uses skills of seeking and receiving feedback.

7. **Manages own career**

Creative and self-reliant in managing own career in constantly changing organisations; can model a career plan along lines of business plan; uses networking skills.

In the chapters which follow we will be exploring these in a way in which you can move to a new level of expertise at work and in your life generally.

Julian, The Work Victim - Revisited

Julian had not assumed the mind set of being *Self Directing*. Although he was an optimistic person and very willing, his assumptions were based more on being led within an organisation which, if not perfect, went a long way towards providing for him the means for his own rapid success. He had not expected the frantic business and seeming chaos of today's modern organisation, and that within this he had to shape his own environment for success.

If Julian changes his approach, there is much he can do to regain control over his own destiny and success. He can ensure that, by questioning well, he can get a clear project brief, including exploring some of the nuances involved, instead of passively taking instructions. If he is not getting the feedback to help him learn rapidly, he can ask his manager for it, and handle the interaction so that it is timely and rewarding both for him and his manager. He can work with clients on a different basis, one of understanding their needs so as to meet them, rather than promoting his own technical expertise. He can take control of his workflow instead of just being carried along with it.

All this, of course, requires a different approach from the initial one which Julian adopted, and where he ended up as a **work victim**. A **Self Directing** approach would be much more profitable for Julian and, if this is carried through with the generic skills associated with it, would position him to get a lot more of what he wants.

Self Directing High Achiever Behaviours

• Really effective people rarely need to have what they have to do explicitly defined for them.

• They take personal responsibility themselves to create the conditions they need to succeed. If they are unclear about what is required, they proactively and skilfully question their manager/clients to get a clear brief.

• If there are conflicting priorities, they negotiate positively to get the best possible result, and because they have thoroughly understood the purpose behind what they are doing, they will add value with suggestions and ideas for improvements.

• They take control of their workload. Because they keep track of their commitments and use positive negotiation to establish priorities, they are reliable in delivering what they have promised.

• High achievers also create their own learning opportunities, such as seeking feedback, and they handle their mistakes in a mature fashion which adds to their credibility. Consequently they develop clear knowledge of their own strengths and weaknesses, and an understanding of how to use their abilities to maximum effect.

• They have the confidence to use their initiative in unclear or risky areas, but are also aware of when they need help and are not afraid to ask for this.

• In addition, the best performers have considerable savvy. They have a solid understanding of commercial needs and priorities, and are keenly aware of the wider implications in the actions they take.

• They have developed an understanding of the organisation they work for and the way things are done there. They are sensitive to the needs of the organisation and others. Much of their success comes from building networks based on good long-term relationships.

• They have a positive approach to overcoming problems, and their willingness to take **Responsible Initiative** for ensuring their won success, demonstrates that they are hassle free achievers and they tend to progress fast.

Chapter 2: Reinforcing & Refining the Self Directing Approach

Changes in the Work Environment

The work environment has changed considerably over recent years making the **Self Directing** approach more important than ever. Such changes include;

- **Empowerment**
Where greater responsibility is passed 'down the line', requiring people to take more ownership and **Responsible Initiative** in identifying what needs to be done, and then taking appropriate action.
- **Increased Span of Control/Delayering**
This results in there being fewer managers and therefore less availability of their time
- **Service Orientation**
The emphasis now is on meeting clients' expectations and needs, and building productive relationships with them. Technical expertise and knowledge of itself is no longer enough and in fact is just the starting point.
- **Increased Performance Expectations**
Today's organisations have little room for coasting or mediocre performance. Enough to get by is no longer enough, especially in managing your own career.
- **Constant Change**
Requiring continuous learning and new skills.
- **Workforce Flexibility**
This means being able to do a number of things well and adjusting to constantly changing circumstances.
- **Remote Working**
With its greater reliance on self management and direction.

Many **work victims** do not cope well with such changes and revert to playing the 'ain't it awful' game, blaming others, society, the organisation, their manager - whatever. They use their energy to reinforce their feeling of powerlessness. Others, like King Canute and the tides, are realistic about the reality of givens, and harness their energy to manager their situation and environment within these realities, and concentrate on the considerable amount they can influence.

It often happens that many of the restraints people put on themselves are self imposed, and stem from the frame of mind, or attitude, with which they perceive the situation. For example, with two people experiencing the same difficult work situation, one's view might be...
'Life is a rat race, I'm always trying to catch up, meet deadlines which aren't important but just routine. So even though I'm nervous and tense, I'm also bored a lot of the time.'
The other person says...
'I'm almost never bored. Even when there's something I have to do that doesn't strike me as interesting at first, usually I find it worthwhile in a way that teaches me something and enables me to shape a future and productive work life for myself.'

As a test of how you see your general situation, ask yourself the question 'How can I succeed when...' then list the things that are getting in your way..
....
Be honest with yourself. When you review your responses again later you may view them as problems, factors or restraints, rather than givens.

IN OTHER WORDS, YOU HAVE A CHOICE!

Personal Power

Power is a term much associated with negative connotations, eg Hitler, in the sense of its potential to do harm, oppress, etc. Yet power is the mainspring of making positive things happen which benefit all. Without a power source, very little is likely to be achieved, for good or ill. Powerlessness, the feeling of having no control of events, or choice, is a state which generates much stress, anxiety and de-spiritedness, as well as creating low self esteem.

Within organisations, there are many sources of power, position power, role power, power based on knowledge, information, money, charisma, influence power. Sometimes, any maybe more outside work, physical and sometimes sexual power can be added to the mix.

Self Directing people have access to a large source of power. This is **PERSONAL POWER**, carried within themselves. **Personal Power** differs because it is based on the individual, not the role, 'uniform' or organisation. It comes from a set of skills used with **Responsible Initiative**. So it is founded on both a state of mind and a set of skills, to follow things through. This 'can do' attitude carries through to successful completion by the tools to make the right things happen. Of course the attitude and skills feed upon themselves - an increase in one results in a corresponding increase in the other.

Self Directing people are not powerless, rather they use their own **Personal Power** to manage their own environment towards a better outcome. Most people have much more **Personal Power** than they realise. They just need to get in touch with it, that's all, and use it through some of the focused skills we shall be exploring shortly. They create **EM**-powerment as opposed to disem-powerment.

In today's organisational world **Personal Power** is replacing the 'command and control' and hierarchical based power that managers traditionally exercised. The additional bonus of getting in touch with and exercising your **Personal Power** is how it can improve the richness of life generally.

*Today, success hinges
on the ability to influence
people to achieve common goals
and purposes. This power to influence
is personal effectiveness. It is the
new power of competence. Such
power is based on the person,
not their position.
It is …*

PERSONAL POWER

Removing Self-Imposed Barriers

A further way of seeing what **Self Directing** people are all about is in the way they approach many of the restraints we can put on ourselves. Some of these have been referred to already, but it is worth looking at them again in a new light.

Perfect Manager

There isn't one. This is not heresy but reality. Waiting for the perfect manager to come along to allow you to grow to your full potential is like waiting for a lottery win. Sometimes your manager will be good, other times less so. Instead of just being a passive respondent in the situation, **Self Directing** people use their skills to **Manage their Manager**. They do this by asking themselves questions like:

'What does my manager want?'
'What annoys my manager?'
'What makes my manager feel positive?'
'What is it that my manager really appreciates?'

This is not a take-over bid, but simply a way of recognising and harnessing the strengths in your manager and finding ways to cope with his/her weaknesses so you can achieve the best possible job, and achieve what you want.

There will be the opportunity for you to think about and answer the above questions in Chapter 5.

Perfect Organisation

Again, there isn't one. **Self Directing** people make best use of the environment they are in. They decide what is important, rather than trying to 'slay every dragon', and shape their own environment to get it.

Examples are:

- *Not getting feedback?* <u>Ask for it</u>.
- *Swamped with inappropriate work?* <u>Negotiate priorities.</u>
- *Interrupted every five minutes so you can't get on with things?* <u>Create disturb and don't disturb zones</u>.
- *Want to stretch your wings and try out your management ability?* <u>Ask to lead a project</u>.

Perfect Colleagues

It matters to you that you do a successful job, on time, but this is dependent on others, and somehow there is always a problem and you get the blame for poor delivery. **Self Directing** people do not accept this, neither do they whinge about it, they anticipate the problem, work out what needs to be done, make positive suggestions to their manager and take responsibility for implementing what is agreed.

Perfect Clients

The client seems to respect your expertise but somehow you end up jumping through hoops because they do not seem to know what they want, and the job ends up by satisfying no-one completely, including yourself.

Self Directing people take responsibility for clearly establishing what the client wants at the outset so they can deliver well. They also proactively build up good, productive relationships with them which develop into strategic partnership. They see the world from the client's perspective, not just from their own technical specialism.

Perfect You

Sad to say, you too are unlikely to be perfect! You will have strengths and corresponding weaknesses, and knowing and recognising them helps. The good news is that you can be better, which is what the quest of **Self Directing** people is all about. They take responsibility for their own continuous learning and improvements.

We also may have 'booby trapped' ourselves by carrying around assumptions or 'life scripts' from the past. It is useful to review these and test them out by revisiting the question *'How can I succeed when…?'* (page 18).

Are these restraints self-imposed or real? How would other people deal with them?

Emotional Intelligence

In recent years a stream of research has emerged on Emotional Intelligence (Goleman) which has had a striking impact on management thinking and practice.

The thinking is that there are three domains of excellence:

Intellectual	as supposedly measured by IQ
Expertise	practical intelligence, technical expertise and experience
Emotional	emotional and interpersonal intelligence

There are relationships between these three, for example, **Emotional Intelligence** skills do have a connection with <u>Intellectual</u> ones. Top performers have both. The aptitude for success starts with intellectual horsepower, but people need emotional competence too to release the full potential of their talent.

In today's world, <u>Expertise</u> is seen to be a baseline competence needed to get the job done. However, in addition to <u>Expertise</u>, how the job is done through the other (**Emotional Intelligence**) competencies determines performance. It is about being able to translate <u>Expertise</u> to something relevant and useful. For example, while one computer programmer relates only to his/her 'techy expertise', another more successful one will be additionally skilled in relating to their client's needs.

Emotional Intelligence is not the same as 'emotional competence', competence is the learned application of this form of competence. What comes out of the research, very clearly, is that it is the emotional competence skills, underpinned by the baseline <u>Expertise</u> ones, which leads to excellence and superior performance. The nature of what is required depends on the particular job; the more senior it is, the more they are likely to be required, but even at a junior level they make a significant difference.

It is no wonder then that modern recruitment practice establishes, and takes for granted, academic, intellectual and technical ability, and looks for the personal qualities, eg initiative, adaptability, etc, of emotional competence.

There is a clear, supporting correlation between the **Key Attitude** and **Skills** of **Self Directing** people and emotional competence. The seven key skills are generic ones, applicable along the spectrum of **Emotional Intelligence**.

The research demonstrated that the 'value added' of people with high emotional competence was:

Low Complexity Jobs - eg Operators/Clerks

> Top 1% was 3 times more productive than bottom 1%

Medium Complexity Jobs - eg Sales Clerk/Mechanic

> Top 1% was 12 times more productive than bottom 1%

High Complexity Jobs - eg Insurance Salespeople/Account Managers/Lawyers/Doctors

> Top 1% was 2.3 times more productive than average ranking performers

Emotional Intelligence is ...

Not about:

'Being nice'	but	**'being real' appropriately**
'Letting it all hang out'	but	**managing feelings and expressing them appropriately**
'Gender stereotypes or advantages'	but	**recognising that both sexes have strengths & weaknesses**
'Having a fixed attitude'	but	**development over a lifetime**

The **Emotional Intelligence** qualities identified in the Goleman's research are shown below. Some are innate qualities while others need to be developed from potential competence (through training and application). If they appear intimidating in their comprehensiveness, remember that not all jobs require the full range, and that the **Seven Key Skills** provide a generic set as a platform for enhancing professional excellence.

Personal Competence
How we manage ourselves

Self Awareness - knowing own preferences and intuitions
- Emotional awareness
- Accurate self-assessment
- Self-confidence

Self Regulation - managing own internal states and impulses
- Self-control
- Trustworthiness
- Conscientiousness
- Adaptability
- Innovation

Motivation - emotional tendencies that guide us to reach our goals
- Achievement drive
- Commitment
- Initiative
- Optimism

Social Competence
How we handle relationships

Empathy - awareness of other's feelings, needs and concerns
- Understanding others
- Developing others
- Service orientation
- Leveraging diversity
- Political awareness

Social Skills - skill at inducing desirable responses in others
- Influence
- Communication
- Conflict management
- Leadership
- Change catalyst
- Building bonds
- Collaboration and co-operation
- Team capabilities

Fine Tuning 'Independence to Interdependence' Attitudes

Another perspective on the **Self Directing** frame of mind comes from the OK Corral. This is a model derived from the theories of Transactional Analysis. It is a useful anchor when you need to understand why an individual is responding to you in a particular way, and what attitude you need to adopt to best handle the situation.

From an early age, people develop a view of their own worth and tend to take "life positions" relative to other people. Life positions develop from experiences, particularly those during childhood, and affect the way people feel, act and relate to others.

The OK Corral Model is concerned with two basic views which an individual will have in mind when dealing with another person.

Firstly how I view myself:

I'm OK	*My self esteem is reasonably high; I feel comfortable with this environment; I feel able to cope*
I'm not OK	*I'm uncomfortable dealing with this sort of issue; I don't feel I have the necessary skills*

It goes without saying that whilst I am sorting out my own underlying attitude to me, I am also viewing you, the other person. I am dealing with you in one of two ways:

You're OK	*You have a right to your opinions; you are essentially decent; you have a contribution to make*
You're not OK	*You never listen; you are wrong; your won't win this one*

The combination of my view of me, and my view of you, give the possibility of four positions, or attitudes as shown on the following page. Each position is typified by particular types of behaviour.

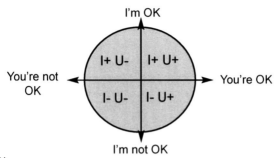

I'm OK

I+ U-   I+ U+

You're not
OK

You're OK

I- U-   I- U+

I'm not OK

I+ U-

If this is your underlying attitude then your behaviour will indicate a feeling of superiority; either through an aggressive stance or alternatively an over-protective parental approach. This is likely to provoke resistance, aggressiveness or dependence from the other party.

I- U-

This attitude is very commonly held by those experiencing change. It manifests itself in a suspicious and often hostile approach to others with an underlying feeling of 'Why bother - it will not make any difference anyway'. To be on the receiving end of this type of behaviour can be frustrating and exhausting, and requires considerable effort to deal with it appropriately.

I- U+

If you are viewing life from this position on the **OK Corral**, it is likely that your self-esteem has taken a knock; you are susceptible to being rescued by the other person who is OK in your mind. Behaviour emanating from here is non-assertive and often yielding, which in turn can lead to a further dip in your self-esteem. An interesting factor about those who often inhabit this quadrant is the lightning switch they can make to I+U-. When the final straw is delivered the method of dealing with it is often an extremely aggressive approach which surprises all parties.

I+U+

This is the most productive position to occupy, whenever possible. Behaviours are assertive but warm, and the underlying attitude is one of positive regard and trust, even when delivering bad news or a potentially unpleasant message. Your expectations of the other person are consistently high; when expectations are high; and supported by positive regard and genuine behaviour, the chances of those expectations being met are significantly increased. Being on the receiving end of I+U+ type behaviours is irresistible; in time, the other party will join you in that quadrant.

(See table)

In terms of the **OK Corral**, the **Self Directing** concept aligns most closely with the **I+U+** quadrant. But this is not the end of the story. People who are **Independent**, rather than truly **Interdependent**, may operate in an **I+U+** fashion in that they engage with other people's needs, but they do not do so in a way which achieves the most productive results.

This is particularly so when there are difficulties in the relationship. Remember the set of characteristics of **Responsible Initiative** include:

• <u>Taking others' needs into account</u> (this does not mean slavishly following them)
• <u>Taking the longer view</u>, by working to make the project, unit or company a success rather than just concentrating on your own work

How basic attitude influences behaviour;

A person when their basic attitude is:	Communicates	Handles disagreements	Solves problems	Gives feedback	Accepts feedback	Feels to others
I'm OK You're OK	Openly	By seeking clarification and mutual resolution	By consulting others and trusting self	Assertively, tactfully and explicitly	Readily and with gratitude, takes action	Equal
I'm OK You're not OK	Aggressively	By placing the blame on others	By unilaterally rejecting others' ideas looking for win/lose	Harshly, by attaching the blame to the participant	Argumentatively, challenging every point	Superior
I'm not OK You're OK	Defensively Self-deprecatingly	By perceiving differences as evidence of inadequacy	By relying almost completely on others	Hesitatingly and with no clarity	Timidly and unquestioningly	Inferior
I'm not OK You're not OK	With hostility Abruptly	By escalating the conflict and involving a third party	By giving in to the problem	Half-heartedly by disowning the feedback and blaming the process	Passively unwillingly looking to blame others	Alienated

What often makes the difference between the **Independent I+U+** and the **Interdependent I+U+** is ...

POSITIVE REGARD & GENUINENESS

Research shows very clearly that effective counsellors need to have two characteristics before they can help their clients. If they do not display these characteristics, then their clients will not respond to them. These findings are extremely relevant to the way in which you discuss with someone their job performance and help them to improve.

The two characteristics are:

Positive Regard

which means having respect for the other person as an individual, and a positive belief in them as a person

Genuineness

which means that you are able to express your own feelings and tell the truth about your reaction to another person's behaviour. It means being direct, open and honest with the other person

Without these underlying characteristics or attitudes, you are unlikely to cause the other person to change and enhance their performance. Also, without them, the interaction is likely to be experienced as false, patronising or manipulative. With them however, not only is the process destined to go well, but the interaction does not have to be technically perfect in order to be a success. In other words:

• The underlying attitudes of **Positive Regard** and **Genuineness** are even more important than the skills of conducting the discussion

• Without them you will have little real influence on other people, particularly those whose performance you wish to help to improve significantly

Maintaining Positive Regard

Sometimes it is not easy to maintain **Positive Regard**. In situations where such a difficulty can be anticipated, it is useful to prepare for the meeting with the individual by thinking about them in the following ways, which will help maintain your **Positive Regard**:

• Identify some of their strengths - not just their weaknesses
• Develop a vision of them performing at their best
• Remember that everyone has reasons for behaving the way they do
• Think back to a time when you felt good about them

Be tough with them if necessary, but do so out of **Positive Regard**. In difficult circumstances it may pay you to confront the other person with your feelings about what they are doing; this is part of being **Genuine**.

Being Genuine

As well as having **Positive Regard** for their clients, research has shown clearly that effective counsellors also have a high degree of **Genuineness**. **Genuineness** means expressing your own feelings and telling the truth about your reaction to the behaviour of the other person. It means being direct, open and honest.

Again this is common sense. It is better to engage with the other person directly, as a human being, and not hide behind the façade of being the perfect manager, always in control, measured and dispassionate. It is about being straight with the other person.

Clearly this does not mean losing your temper or over-reacting. Rather it is concerned with having sufficient **Positive Regard** for the other person to 'tell it like it is' concentrating on what they do (the behaviour) that is causing good or poor performance. Remember, **Positive Regard** values the person as a person, but not necessarily their behaviour.

Confronting someone in this way is a particularly powerful way to get them to change and improve their performance. For example:

'Bill, it makes me angry and sad that I feel I can't rely on your work. Every time I give you a job to do you do it willingly and turn it around quickly. I really appreciate that. But what gets me is that there is always a silly mistake in your work. It spoils a good job and it's a shame. What makes me most angry is that I've raised this with you before and you haven't done anything about it. So come on Bill, get it sorted, I know you can do it. Check your own work before you pass it on to me and you'll be doing a great job.'

If you keep your feelings bottled up they will leak out anyway through body language and may be misinterpreted. Alternatively, they will come out at a later stage with irritation or anger. Also if the interaction is not open and honest or worse still is manipulative, then the other person will soon sense this. You can rarely keep feelings as hidden as you think you can!

Genuineness is part of **Positive Regard** and it is not possible to have **Positive Regard** without being **Genuine**. Both are essential attitudes for feedback, for effective performance reviews and for improvement to take place.

It is very similar to a view of **Assertion**:

Assertion
        is about standing up for your own needs while
        respecting those of the other person

Aggression
        is concerned solely with your own needs

Non-Assertion
        implies neglecting your own needs and/or going
        passively along with those of the other person

Passivity	**ASSERTION**	Aggression
←		→
Other person's needs		Your needs

Chapter 3: Questioning & Listening

It is astonishing and sad how **Dependent** people miss out on so many opportunities for richness in their personal lives and in the workplace. They put themselves in a powerless, 'Can't Do' situation because they rely on 'they', whoever 'they' are, to provide them with important information and direction. It is as if they need to be continuously spoon-fed with information or the help they need.

People who use initiative irresponsibly are not bothered by information; they work on the fallacy that they have somehow guessed correctly the information they need. **Self Directing** people however know when to proactively obtain information. They know that the solution to many of their issues is to **ASK**.

It used to be said that 'those who ask, don't get'. This was an admonition used frequently in childhood. Yet, in adulthood at least, the reverse is true, those who don't ask, don't get, those who ask often do.

For Example:
If your manager or client is not being very clear what he or she wants
> **Ask, appropriately, until you have a clear mental picture of what is wanted**

If you do not have the background information to do your work well
> **Ask for it**

If you are not getting the feedback or help to learn a new skill quickly
> **Ask for it**

If you want to attend a training programme, but you have not been invited yet
> **Ask to attend**

While taking **Responsible Initiative** is the keystone attitude to **Personal Excellence** and success, **Questioning** and **Listening** are probably the most important skills. More, these skills impact other ones, such as Positive Negotiation and Managing your own Learning and Career.

So what is the big deal? Everyone uses **Questioning** and **Listening** don't they; they have been doing it all their lives?

Self Directing people have learned some refined skills, skills which enable them to obtain quality information quickly and well, to hear and absorb it, and to use this as the springboard for effective, purposeful action. These skills we will be exploring. They benefit people both in their work and personal lives

Consider some situations where using **Questioning** and **Listening** well will enable you to be even more successful, such as **Questioning** to …

• <u>Find out information</u> - to generate quality solutions, achieve first time, without difficulties and false starts along the way

• <u>'Selling to need' and provide what the client really wants</u> - which starts by finding out what the client really wants

• <u>Take charge of your own development</u> - through, for example, tapping into the skills of those around you, getting quality feedback, exploring new possibilities

• <u>Build relationships</u> - through understanding other's points of view, establishing contact with them and mutual positive regard

• <u>Get what you want</u> - things you want will not automatically just come your way. Asking, eg 'Can I' is both a polite and assertive way of stating a request rather than a demand

Good **Questioning** starts of course with good **Listening**.

It may be no accident that we have two ears and one mouth, which, as they saying goes, should be used in proportion!

Active and Effective Listening

Effective Listening is not a passive skill. If you wish to really understand what is being said, explore further feelings and attitudes or encourage the person to say more, then there are certain attitudes and behaviours you need to demonstrate.

1. Attitude

You need to be genuinely interested in what is being said and who is saying it, and you need to have Positive Regard for the speaker and to be prepared to empathise with them. Empathising does not necessarily mean agreeing with them, but understanding and respecting where they are coming from.

2. Concentration

Good listening is tiring because it requires you to make an effort to get beyond the words that are being said. You need to become attuned to the feelings and thoughts that lie behind the words. This is possible provided that you concentrate on the listening process and do not allow yourself to be distracted, either by outside events or by your own thought process.

It is all too easy to allow yourself to start judging what is being said, or to start phrasing your next intervention or question. Whenever possible, just allow yourself to absorb the content like a sponge, storing away any points which you perhaps need to explore further at the appropriate time.

3. Non-Verbal Behaviours

Appropriate non-verbal behaviours show the speaker that you are genuinely listening. The following list briefly explains the non-verbal signals that are demonstrated by the best listeners. When used naturally, they can help generate the desired feelings of understanding, empathy and non-evaluative acceptance.

• **Posture** - alert and attentive without invading the speaker's personal space. Often the listener's posture will mirror the speaker's when active listening is taking place.

• **Eye contact** - the speaker needs you to be there with eye contact when they look at you; but not boring into them and not a glassy eyed stare! Many speakers look away from you while they are collecting their thoughts. This is not to do with 'shiftiness' and it is important that you are 'there' when they return to you.

• **Nodding and 'grunting'** - to show understanding and encourage the speaker to say more. A limited use of nodding and 'uh-huhs' is useful; too much and you give the impression of wanting to hurry the speaker along (or become irritating to them).

• **Appropriate facial expressions** - if you are in there with them, allow empathy to show in your face. A smile, a frown or look of concern at the right time is very powerful in demonstrating you are listening. As an example watch a group of men hearing about a friend's experience of a vasectomy - much wincing!!

4. Paraphrasing

Active Listening does not mean keeping totally silent. You may need to check your understanding of what has been said, or whether you have accurately construed their meaning. Rephrase what the speaker has said in your own words, use phrases like, 'As I understand it, what you're saying is...' or 'Do you mean that...' Avoid repeating their words parrot fashion.

5. Reflecting Underlying Feelings

As stated earlier, truly **Effective Listening** goes beyond simply hearing the spoken word, in that it is perceptive to the feelings involved. Test the accuracy of your perception with phrases such as 'I suppose that must have been awkward for you' or 'I guess that really annoyed you'. If you are right the speaker is encouraged by your understanding and feels able to say more. If you are wrong, it can provoke further clarification along the lines of 'I wasn't annoyed, more frustrated by what had happened' or 'Annoyed! - I was absolutely steaming!'.

6. Summarising

If you are listening to something very detailed or complex, it may be necessary for you to get the speaker to pause so that you can break up what you are hearing into manageable chunks. Use phrases like 'Hang on, what we've got so far is...' or 'OK, so the order of events was...' This ensures that you have picked up and stored away, in digestible amounts, what is being said and allows you to concentrate on the rest without embarking on major feats of memory!

7. Spotting Signals

Occasionally the speaker will drop signals into the conversation, which can be particularly useful. If you can, pick up on them and explore more thoroughly.

• **Trailing sentences** - look for the 'trailing off' at the end of a sentence, it can often speak volumes. For example, 'How is the team doing?' 'Well they are all working hard on their individual work...' The tone of voice could well be giving you the clue that whilst the individual work is fine, teamwork may be a problem.

• **Stopping for a reaction** - it is natural for the speaker to stop when they have just made a significant point. They are often looking to you for a response, which will encourage them to go on. If you leap in with your own views at that point, you may miss their signal. Instead say something like, 'OK that sounds important, say some more' or 'I've got some thoughts on that which we'll come back to - I'm interested to hear more from you on that'.

• **The throwaway line** - listen particularly to things people say as they are about to leave. These may be things they have been trying to get round to saying but haven't found the opportunity to raise them.

• **Key words** - listen for key words, possibly words that they emphasise, which warrant some further exploration. For example, 'I've had some/little difficulty in coming to terms with the new system but they are only minor concerns - nothing to worry about'.

Active Listening does not include probing questions of a cross-examination type such as 'Why did you do that?' or 'What are you going to do about it?' These types of questions cause the control of the discussion to shift away from the speaker and, therefore potentially useful information may be lost.

It is inevitable that you will need to ask some questions at some stage but not at the expense of the speaker's flow. Avoid using their words like a flow of traffic, waiting for a gap so you can cross with your own questions. Go with the flow and suspend judgement until the traffic has passed.

Levels of Listening

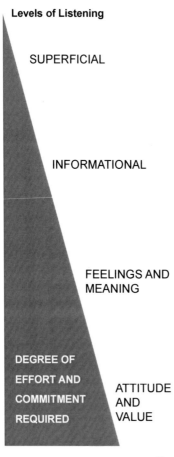

Levels of Listening	The Listening Process
SUPERFICIAL	Person hears what is being said but as if from a distance. Does just enough to maintain the conversation, but does not get involved with or committed to the content of what is being said.
INFORMATIONAL	Person hears what is being said and selects and seeks facts and information. The content of what is being said is heard but the feelings which accompany are either avoided or consciously heard.
FEELINGS AND MEANING	The person hears not only the information, but the feelings which accompany the information. They actively seek clarification and understanding of what is being felt and what that means for the person talking.
ATTITUDE AND VALUE	Having established the informational content and the feelings concerned, the listener then actively explores why the speaker feels the way they do.

DEGREE OF EFFORT AND COMMITMENT REQUIRED

Effective Questioning

Effective Questioning requires a number of techniques, which with practice become everyday skills exercised naturally. Like breathing, questioning is an everyday part of life, and the correct breathing techniques help enormously when carrying out difficult exercise. So it is with questioning.

We shall be looking at more advanced questioning techniques later. Let's start with the basics. Common types of questions:

Open Questions:
which can't be answered by a simple yes or no are often preceded by a What, Where, When, How, etc, and which generate much information, For example: *Why do you think that? How would you approach the problem? Where would be a good place to meet?*

Closed Questions:
which limit the range of answers to a yes or no. For example: *Do you want to take the job on? Is this all right by you? Shall we meet at …?*

There are of course other types of question commonly used, some of which have the disadvantage shown over the page. The building blocks of good technique however are open and closed questions.

Putting Open and Closed Questions to Work

Open Questions encourage the other person to talk, and are useful in explaining and gathering information. Sometimes the answers are not in the direction the questioner intended, or are so rich in information that the questioner becomes overwhelmed or drifts off the point particularly with talkative people. The questioner can feel out of control, and open-ended questioning can be quite time consuming.

Non-Useful Types of Questions

Question	Useful	Not Useful
Leading *'You do play golf, don't you?'* Invariably leads to an answer you expect	For gaining possible acceptance of your view	For getting sound, quality information.
Multiple String of questions joined together	Never	Always
Hypothetical *'What would you do if...'* Posing hypothetical situations in the future	Rarely. Much better to explore real situations which the jobholder has experienced.	Almost always. Answers are hypothetical too.
Judging *'When was the last time you did something positive to help the team as a whole?'* Questions which contain judgement that the jobholder is stupid, lazy poorly regarded etc.	Never	Always

Closed Questions on the other hand close the person down - eg 'Did you agree with that?' - and can establish specific points and facts. Although seemingly time efficient, they do not explore the gaps between 'black' and 'white', and also are not appropriate in **emotionally** charged areas.

What often happens in practice is that an open (**Divergent**) question is asked which produces a richness of information, which the questioner has difficulty in dealing with and closes that part of the conversation down with a closed (**Convergent**) question. This is because the questioner is busy listening and at the same time trying to phrase the next question, or feels out of control of the situation in that he or she wants to bring the conversation back on track. It is also more difficult to construct open questions that closed ones.

However, if a questioning technique is used which starts with an open question, the response to which is followed through and explored appropriately, with the conversation then moved on or refocused to the next issue, much more can be effectively, and pleasurably, achieved.

Quality Information is achieved by introducing two other types of questions, **Probing** and **Refocusing**, in ways we shall now explore. Thereafter there is a further refinement of technique which take these principles further, **Critical Incident Interviewing**.

Probing and Refocusing for Clarification

There are three types of questions or questioning techniques that are effective in obtaining quality information, but not so often used. Yet these three can make all the difference in both getting a quality result and in the good flow of interaction. They are sometimes known as 'consultant' questions.

1. Probing questions, used to draw someone out without leading them in any way.

2. **Refocusing questions**, used to move people on to a different subject, with their permission. **Probing** and **Refocusing** are best used in conjunction with each other. Typically the process is an **Open** question, the response to which is explored by probing, followed by refocusing.

3. **Critical Incident** technique, is a refinement of **Probing** and **Refocusing**, and will be dealt with later.

As we have already discussed, most people rely on **Open** or **Closed** questions, ie **Divergent** or **Convergent** ones, and that between these two extremes is the territory of quality information. The more usual sequence of questioning is an open one followed by a closed one. There are a number of reasons for this:

• Concern at being experienced as being a harsh interrogator.
• The difficulty of thinking up good questions, particularly open-ended ones, gives the focus needed on listening to the other person. It is not easy to listen well while wondering 'What is the next question I am going to ask?'
• Concern about getting stuck on a particular questioning line, and not being able to move the other person on without seeming unsympathetic or breaking up the flow.
• Lack of knowledge or skill about the technique of **Probing** and **Refocusing**.

The way to overcome all this is firstly to develop a 'bank' of all-purpose 'probes' and 'refocusing' questions (see examples listed over). It is important that these are translated into a form which fits you. With this 'bank' you are positioned to use the technique and develop the skills, and you will feel more comfortable and confident about probing appropriately. You will also be able to concentrate on the other person's replies, without concerns about framing the next question getting in the way.

For data collection, a good general rule is to start with an open question, followed by a couple of probes and then refocus, so the process can start again. The number of probes used will, of course, vary according to the situation, but too many or too few both have their dangers. The biggest danger of all though is to not use probes at all - or badly - when trying to get quality information.

Examples of General Purpose 'Probes'

- **To keep the person talking**
  'OK?'
  'Could you expand on that?'
  "Could you say a bit more about that?'

- **To get concrete examples**
  'Can you give me an example?'
  'What did she/he actually do?'
  'Are there any more instances like that you could tell me about?'

- **To find out feelings and reactions**
  'How do you feel about that?'
  'What did you think about that?'
  'How did you cope with that?'

Examples of Refocusing Questions

- *'Can we move on to look at ... now?'*
- *'I'd also like to talk about ... if that's OK?'*
- *'OK, I understand what you are saying, but let's think about the future now.'*
- *'What do you think you could do to overcome that problem?'*

Critical Incident Interviewing

This technique of questioning is a particularly powerful way of collecting data, and can be used for a variety of purpose. It is very structured and therefore lends itself to those situations where it is necessary to get meaningful information in a relatively short time.

The interview can, by using the basic steps, encourage the interviewee to tap into real events and their experience of them, and avoid hypothetical answers coloured by what the interviewee thinks the interviewer wants to hear.

The information derived using this process is genuine and is likely to be specific and explicit, thereby providing maximum benefit.

To illustrate the process the following is an example of someone needing to gather data from a colleague (A) on the performance of a third party (X).

1. Establish the Framework - Explain that you need to elicit some information about X and that you would value A's thoughts. Check that A has had dealings with X in recent months and, if possible, establish the frequency - eg once in the last six months, or every month for the last year, etc.

2. Create Real Recollections - Ask A to think back over his dealings with X. Establish if possible, two instances that were good, had a positive outcome, produced the required end result, went well etc. It is not necessary for A to tell you what these were, it is just for A to bring these to the forefront of his mind.

Next ask A to think of an instance in his dealings with X that was less good, less productive, etc.

3. Establish the Differences - Starting with the positive instances, ask how they differed from the less positive example. Allow A to continue and then return to one difference and establish:

• *'What did X actually do?'*
• *'What did X actually say?'*
• Probe for specific examples of behaviour that contributed to the positive view held by A

Having explored three or four positive areas, ask A about the less positive instances. How were they difference from those already discussed. Again, allow a free reign, and then return to each topic to establish specific examples.

4. Summarise - After each topic summarise what you have noted down, then add any additional information or clarification that A gives you following your summary.

There is no need for great originality during this process. If necessary, use the same question structure repeatedly. This is not a gentle conversation over a coffee, but a concentrated (albeit non-threatening) process to obtain maximum information in the minimum time.

By directing the interviewee down the paths of actual experience, and by concentrating on the areas in which you are particularly interested, you make it considerably easier for him to focus on what is real and relevant. The alternative, 'How do you think X has done this year?' leaves A floundering for something to say. When A finally does say something, it is likely to be very general and bland.

As mentioned, the **Critical Incident Interviewing** technique can be used for a variety of purposes:

- Seeking feedback
- Determining expectations and defining levels of performance
- Deriving competencies
- Establishing motivation indicators (through the exploitation of good and bad experiences of previous jobs)
- Selection interviews

For whatever reason you are going to use the process, you will need to spend a little time preparing the questions you will be asking, and the ends of experience/spectrum that you will be exploring. It is desirable to keep it as simple as possible, as it helps to speed the process and prevents the interviewee from getting sidetracked.

As with most skills, your competency and comfort will increase with practice and refinement.

Chapter 4: Positive Negotiation & Influence

Positive Negotiation involves using appropriate **Influencing**. With **Influencing**, most people tend to get into the habit of using perhaps one or two of these styles, rather than having developed the ability to use the whole range, and more, to pick a style which suits the particular situation:

(See tables)

Positive Negotiation and Conflict Management

Negotiation and **Conflict** are an everyday part of working life. By negotiation we are not referring to commercial negotiation such as purchasing, although some of the same principles apply, but to those everyday occurrences where you may encounter different views, priorities, goals etc. This can happen with your manager, colleagues and at home. Rather than 'suffer in silence', or allowing events to prove the other person wrong, or even 'throwing their teddy out of the pram'; **Self Directing** people use **Responsible Initiative** to proactively resolve these issues, both in their own interests and those of the other people concerned.

Examples of such issues include:

- Conflicting priorities in scheduling work

- How to progress certain tasks

- What constitutes a successful project outcome

or

1. Asserting

Characteristics of this Style

- Being clear about communicating your own needs and limits

- Being clear about communicating your goals 'I need X' 'I must have Y'

- Stating needs and repeating statements where necessary (broken record technique)

- Firm Authoritative

Appropriate Use

- Resisting sales pressure

- Representing yourself or your group in a "win:lose" situation

- Where you and the other party have equal power, or where you have authority

2. Persuading

Characteristics of this Style

• Using logical arguments to convince others that your suggestion is the best course of action

• Demonstrating to others that your suggestion will bring benefits to them

• Providing facts and figures to support your arguments

Appropriate Use

• Where you wish to convince others, and bring them to your point of view

• Where others must understand why they are doing what you suggest

• Where you and the other party have equal power, and where it is important to keep a good relationship going

• Where the other party (or parties) is undecided, and open to influence

• Where you are aiming to influence a decision made by your superiors or clients

3. Bridging

Characteristics of this Style

- Emphasising common ground and areas of mutual benefit

- Stressing the areas on which you already agree

- Finding common values and principles and referring to these

- Creating a feeling that 'we are on the same side'; using 'we' and 'our'

Appropriate Use

- Where there is a need for close co-operation and joint working

- Where there is a need to build closeness and mutual dependency

- Where the other person needs support and encouragement

4. Attracting

Characteristics of this Style

• Visioning, painting exciting pictures of possible futures

• Appealing to a common vision of how things could be done

• Using metaphors and examples to illustrate a principle

• Appeal to emotions rather than to logic 'I have a dream'

Appropriate Use

• Where there is a need to excite and energise people

• Where you want to create a strong culture, where others will put themselves out for 'the dream'

• Where you need to sway large groups of people in an inspiring way

• Where you need to appeal from a distance - for example leading from the top where you have little or no contact with individuals you are persuading

5. Moving Away

Characteristics of this Style

• Failing to rise to the bait, allowing inflammatory comments to pass

• Removing yourself from a situation, either temporarily or permanently

• Avoiding a particular person, or seeing them only when necessary

• Saying nothing and accommodating others

• Calling a break to cool down or leaving the room temporarily

Appropriate Use

• When there is conflict over a minor issue, and to confront it would endanger an accord on more important topics

• When petty interpersonal conflict is getting in the way of achievement

• When you have a fundamental difference of opinion with another person and all attempts to resolve it have failed

56

- Which pub to go to

- Whether to have Chinese or Indian Food

- Where to go on holiday

Positive Negotiation is so called because the intent is to have a positive outcome, hopefully a win:win one. This is achievable more often than not. The downside to not entering the reality of positive negotiation is often not successfully achieving; there is less satisfaction and self-esteem, and stress of the passive 'absorb it' kind.

Stress also is an output of **Conflict**, if that conflict is not proactively managed. There are parallels between **Conflict Management** and **Positive Negotiation**. As we shall see, both cannot be avoided, in the workplace at least, what matters is how they are dealt with. Both have the upside of changing the status quo to get a better result. Non self directing approaches mean that one becomes a passive victim of such situations, the **Self Directing** approach provides much more potential for influencing the situation productively.

Negotiating Styles Descriptions

Competing
This represents a battling, hard nosed style, often typical of management and trade union negotiations and husband and wife arguments, with both parties striving hard to achieve their objectives, showing little co-operation towards each other. This style could be justified if, for example, unpopular courses of action such as cost cutting have to be undertaken, or in emergencies when time does not permit other approaches.

Co-operating
This appears the most desirable style to adopt in negotiations where alongside high assertiveness and determination to achieve objectives, high levels of co-operation are displayed in seeking a solution acceptable to all parties. This co-operating style is best illustrated in an ideal situation where two parties who are each pursuing their own, different objectives and advocating different courses of action, talk through issues in constructive, co-operation fashion and develop a new course of action which permits both sets of objectives to be achieved. While generally this is the preferred style for negotiating over major issues, there may be certain situations when, as previously noted, each of the other four styles can be justified.

Compromising
This represents a middle-of-the-road style. The person who adopts this style often enjoys the give and take of the tactics of bargaining in reaching compromised positions. It is often the case, however, that other factors may determine the use of the compromising style. The compromising style may be adopted if the issue under consideration does not justify the use of greater assertion associated with the competing and collaborative approaches. If both parties have roughly equal power and status but are pursuing opposite objectives, then the compromising approach to negotiation may be the only realistic option.

Avoiding

The kind of person who adopts this approach is likely to feel uncomfortable when facing negotiating situations, and prefers to avoid the problem of resolving differences through negotiation. In some situations this may be the right thing to do, if it is felt that the dangers of confronting the differences outweigh the benefits.

Accommodating

This is very much the 'nice guy' approach in which the individual shows a high degree of co-operation towards the other party, but is often ready to yield on objectives, giving way to the other party. This approach could be justified if the issue over which the negotiations are taking place is seen as trivial in importance. By yielding to the other party social credits may be generated, which can be used in subsequent negotiations on more important issues.

Your Preferred Style

It is likely that you will have a preferred style, and a back up one inclining to pursuing your own interests or allowing others' interests to take precedence if your preferred style is not working.

The ideal preferred style of course is **Co-operating**, as this results in a *win:win*. To achieve this requires some 'hard' skills (<u>assertion</u>), as well as some 'soft' ones (<u>listening</u>), used in combination. It also requires the flexibility of problem solving, and using other 'currencies' to trade with than the starting ones.

A common difficulty in the UK particularly is that **Compromise** has a cultural value as a good thing, so it is often seen as a preferred negotiation style. Both parties get something of what they want resulting in a weak *win:win*, and some defusion of conflict. However when compared with the large *win:win* and probable new or creative solutions of **Co-operating**, it is limited in its potential. **Co-operation** in this sense is akin to strategic partnership, more effort initially but with a much bigger payoff. So in many if not most situations it is the preferred initial style, and if your present one is **Compromising** try to shift your horizon and redirect your energy to the **Co-operating** primary style.

Another common cultural difficulty is that **Competing** has a strong value in our society, as it is aligned with winning sports, etc, to the extent it becomes a personal contest, where emotions take over, rather than being concerned with the issues. Being 'beaten' has certain consequences in negotiation for the other party, who will not see it as positive. *Win:lose* outcomes have a habit of being deflected into *lose:lose* ones. Nevertheless, there are times and situations where the particular issue is desperately important for you, that **Competing** as a fall back style when **Co-operating** is not working, is valid. However if it is always your stance in the workplace then it is unlikely to produce consistently good, positive results.

There are times when **Accommodating** is sensible, for example if the issue matters to the other person but is not very important to you. It can also help in building up a fund of goodwill, which can come in useful on future occasions. However, avoid Accommodation if it results from being aggressed upon, this will simply encourage the other person to aggress more, so such aggression has to be dealt with before **Accommodating**. The problem with **Accommodating** if used too often, say as a preferred style, is that you become a 'doormat' where your own needs are not met.

Avoiding as a way of life through a preferred style is not to be recommended as nothing is resolved or achieved, and it reinforces feelings of inadequacy. This is not to say that **Avoiding** at times is not useful. Obvious examples are when you are not in the right mental space or have the time to confront the issue. The important thing is to <u>choose</u> to use the style, rather than just feeling you have 'wimped out'. Not everything in life has to be tacked hard on.

Choice is the operative word when using the styles. The ideal situation is to have a Co-operating *win:win* orientation and the skills to go with this for **Positive Negotiation**, but also to have the other styles flexibly dependent on the situation. For example some issues are too minor to invest time in, or you choose to "gift" them to the other person (<u>Accommodating</u>), or not to involve the family in potentially dangerous situations (<u>Avoiding</u>), or not to have important principles transgressed (<u>Competing</u>), or to get to a quick solution when time is of the essence (<u>Compromising</u>).

Your present style range is likely to be readily known to people you work with, particularly when it comes to fallback styles, which are likely to be either pursuing your won interests or learning theirs. Knowing how the other person is likely to react, and being prepared and able to deal with it is part of **Positive Negotiation**.

Conflict Resolution

Conflict is a daily reality for everyone. Needs and values constantly come into opposition with those of other people. Some conflicts are relatively minor, easy to handle, or capable of being overlooked. Others of greater magnitude however require a strategy for successful resolution if they are not to create a constant tension.

Conflict resolution strategies may be classified into three categories - **Avoidance**, **Defusion** and **Confrontation** as follows:

Avoidance	Some people attempt to avoid conflict situations altogether, or to avoid certain types of conflict. These people tend to repress emotional reactions, look the other way, or leave the situation entirely. Either they cannot face up to such situations, or they do not have the skills to negotiate them effectively. On occasion, avoidance strategies do have a value - where the outcome is simply not worth bothering about, or where a lose:win will be the most probable result. However, they usually do not result in a high level of satisfaction. They tend to leave doubts and fears about meeting the same type of situation in the future, and about such "valued" traits as courage or persistence. Much depends on whether the choice was a conscious one, or whether the remaining feeling is one of lack of resolution.
Defusion	This tactic is essentially a delaying action. Defusion strategies try to cool off the situation, at least temporarily, or to keep the issues so unclear that attempts at resolution are improbable. Resolving minor points while avoiding or delaying discussion of the major problem, postponing a confrontation until a more auspicious time, and avoiding clarification of the salient issues underlying the conflict are examples of defusion. Again, as with avoidance strategies, such tactics work when delay is possible, but they typically result in feelings of dissatisfaction, anxiety about the future, and concerns about oneself.

	The third major strategy involves an actual confrontation of conflicting issues or persons. Confrontation can further be subdivided into power strategies and negotiation strategies. Power strategies include the use of physical force (a punch on the nose, war) and punishment (withholding love, recognition, money). Such tactics are often very effective from the point of view of the 'successful' party in the conflict - he wins, the other person loses. Unfortunately, however, for the loser the real conflict may have only just begun. Hostility and anxiety are the usual by-products of these *win:lose* power tactics.
Confrontation	

Negotiating Strategies and Skills

Successful negotiation requires a set of skills, which can be learned and practised. These skills include:

1. **Diagnosis**: the ability to determine the nature of the conflict

2. **Initiation:** effectiveness in initiating resolution

3. **Listening:** the ability to hear the other's point of view

4. **Problem Solving:** utilising problem solving processes to bring about a decision

1. **Diagnosis**

Diagnosing the nature of a conflict is the starting point in any attempt at resolution through negotiation. The most important issue, which must be decided, is whether the conflict is an 'ideological' (*value*) conflict, or a 'real' (*tangible*) conflict - or a combination of both. Value conflicts are exceedingly difficult to negotiate, and workable solutions are only likely to come from concentrating on the tangible issues or affects of the conflict.

The Israeli-Arab conflict provides a good example of this point. In order to settle the tangible element in the conflict - who gets how much land - ideological differences do not need to be resolved. It is land usage that is in the area of conflict amenable to a negotiated settlement.

The reality often is that neither person needs to change their values to come to a mutually acceptable resolution of the 'real' problem, which is more about what people do (their behaviour). All too often, though, progress gets stuck in the swamp of conflicting values, without the tangible issues being surfaced.

So, having determined whether a conflict is real or a value conflict - if it is to do with values resulting in non-tangible effects on either party, then it is best tolerated. If, however, a tangible effect exists, that element of the conflict should be resolved.

2. Initiation

Another skill necessary to **Conflict Resolution** is effectiveness in raising the issue to initiate a resolution. It is important not to begin by attacking or demeaning the other person. The most effective way to confront the other person is for you to state the tangible effects the conflict has on you. For example, 'I have a problem - due to your stand on hiring women executives, I am unhappy to apply for the supervisory position that I feel I am qualified to handle.' This approach is more effective than saying, 'You male chauvinist pig - you're discriminating against me.' In other words, confrontation is not synonymous with verbal attack.

3. Listening

Once initiation has been made, you must be demonstrably willing to hear the other person's point of view. If your position on the issue is a surprise to the other person, or is not what they were hoping to hear, defensive rebuttals, a 'hard line' approach or explanations can often result. Avoid argument provoking replies at this stage, or defending you, explaining your position or making demands or threats. Instead, concentrate in active listening.

Reflect and paraphrase or clarify the other person's stand. When the other person's position has been interpreted to your satisfaction, then present your own point of view, being careful to avoid value statements and concentrating on tangible outcomes. Usually, when you really listen to the other person, that person is, in turn, more ready to hear another point of view. Of course, if both persons are skilled in active listening, the chances of successful negotiation are much enhanced.

4. Problem Solving

The final skill necessary for successful resolution is the use of the problem solving process to negotiate an outcome. The steps in this process are:

• <u>Clarifying the problem</u>. 'What is the tangible issue?' 'Where does each party stand on the issue?'

• <u>Generating and evaluating a number of possible solutions</u>. Keep problems clear of the values arena, and instead concentrate on actions and behaviour. Be creative and imaginative - this is the way most problems are unblocked.

• Concentrating on achieving a _win:win_ outcome, so that each person gets largely what they want. This does not necessarily need to be a 'weak' _win:win_, that is a compromise. Rather, depending on how well you have listened to the other person to get really clear what is important to them, and on being creative it is often possible to get to a 'third' solution, which is better in quality than the originally proposed ones.

• Making proposals about a solution. A useful technique here, sometimes called 'The Third Party Negotiation', is to propose, say, 'If I do (this), will you do (that)? This again focuses around tangible outcomes or behaviours, not values. It is possible to jointly plan the implementation of the solution and 'contract' with each other to carry it out.

Based on K W Thomas "Conflict and Conflict Management" 1976 , R H Kilmann.

Chapter 5: Managing Your Own Workload

Imagine for a moment that you are leading a work team. Perhaps one member of your team is into **Dependency**, treating you as though you were their mum or dad. They expect you to solve all their problems - work, relationships, their career, whatever. It may be flattering despite being wearisome, and may appeal to some part of you; you may feel a sense of protectiveness towards them. But when there is a need to streamline the department, the cold reality is they will be an early candidate for removal rather than progression.

Another team member might take lots of initiative, but too often wrongly placed causing immense difficulties for you and the others. This team member may have many admirable qualities - energy, enthusiasm, drive - but it is like managing a loose cannon or rebellious teenager. You cannot yet trust them to do the right things.

The majority of your team are good workers, conscientious, reasonable and courteous with other people. However, when compared with the perhaps one or two higher performers you have, there is a crucial difference.

The difference is that the higher performers operate with **Responsible Initiative** and are **Self Directing** in managing their work. They anticipate problems and find solutions to them, knowing when to involve or consult their manager. They work proactively and productively with other people. They are clear about what needs to be achieved and manage their own workload and deadlines. They add value rather than just completing a task. They are of course technically accomplished, but they are far more than that as they are able to translate this to value added outcomes. They have **nous**.

What does nous mean? It involves seeing the work carried out not as something isolated in itself but part of a bigger picture, which not only gives it meaning and connection to the whole, but also where opportunities are presented. For example, tasks are generally one of three kinds: Operational, Tactical, Strategic.

Operational - The implementation or execution of bits of work, sometimes routine and 'proceduralised'. All of our work involves some of this, sometimes it is the main part. The timescale is short term.

Tactical - Organisational and planning how the work is to be done and the resources required. It involves co-ordinating and project managing it. The timescale is medium term.

Strategic - Seeing the wider meaning and ramifications of the task and how it fits into the 'big picture'. In this way dovetailing can be better achieved and new opportunities taken advantage of - perhaps for improved methods, outcomes, customer satisfaction or increased business.

The **Self Directing Professional** may be at the early stages of their career. What marks them out is the ability to not only carry out the operational part of their work competently, and to organise it, but to do so in the context of seeing those tasks in a wider, strategic sense. They know how their work fits into the jigsaw of the whole, and in a way, where difficulties and problems are anticipated and managed, and importantly where value is created. This is nous!

Getting Clarity on What is Required

This is of course the essential starting point, particularly with less routine tasks and in undertaking a project, otherwise it will be a 'stab in the dark' or at best an educated guess. Focus on the outcome of what is required and the definition of success by getting a clear briefing, if necessary using the **Questioning** techniques described in chapter 3.

Managing Your Manager

This is not heresy - it is an unspoken reality. The relationship is a two-way street if you are a **Self Directing Professional**.

What are your manager's (or client's) wants and needs, fears and hopes, foibles and characteristics? If they constantly need to know how a job is progressing, whether for operational purposes or because that is the way they are, take the initiative to speak to them, to give a short progress report at sufficient intervals to keep them off your back. They will soon learn to be reassured. If something happens that they will be questioned about, let them know rather than allow them to walk into a 'booby trap'. Deliver on promises made. Above all, when there is a problem they should know about, think through some possible solutions.

Managing My Manager Checklist

Complete the following checklist to analyse your manager's behaviour and work out how to get on with him or her better. It should also give you some ideas about how to reward your manager when s/he does things which you find helpful and would like him/her to do more of.

What does my manager want?
• *What makes him/her feel good themselves?*
• *What are some of the driving forces in his/her life?*
• *What is it that tends to get him/her annoyed or upset?*

What behaviour annoys my manager?

What behaviour makes my manager feel positive?

What rewards would my manager like?

Know the Culture of Your Organisation

Simply put, this is the 'way things are done around here'. Each organisation is different, perhaps in a subtle way, but the differences are still important. Culture involves not only what is done, but how it is done - the rules of engagement so to speak. Good carpenters are adept at working with the grain but know how to deal with tricky obstacles such as a knot or hitherto hidden nails.

Recognise & Manage Your Workload Profile

First we have to recognise some problems which might be quite 'deep seated' and are connected with a mindset of **Dependency** and **Counter Dependency**, rather than **Self Directing** attitudes. These are:

Ain't it awful	Where every problem is blamed on someone else - the organisation, boss, co-workers, the system or whatever - with no responsibility accepted for own capability.
Harried	Taking on everything, volunteering to come early and work late, undertaking weekend assignments, acting like superman/woman and getting worn down. The pay-off is being able to cash in on favourite feelings of being depressed and put upon.
Wooden leg	Surely you can't expect much from me when I have such a handicap - ie wrong sex, wrong size, wrong race, wrong background, wrong state of health, etc.
See how hard I tried	Dont blame me if things turn out wrong, after all, see how hard I tried (the underlying agenda is to 'try' but not achieve).

Workload Control – Managing Stress

Clearly staying in control of your own workload is a key part of being **Self Directing**, and rushing round in a panic, failing to deliver what has been promised, creating more problems rather than finding solutions, is hardly a recipe for success. Neither is it helpful in avoiding unnecessary stress. It is different, in fact, from the purposeful and effective performance of those who achieve reliably and well. Unless one is addicted to self-induced stress, being out of control is not a good place to be and has consequences for how you are regarded, your capability for possible promotion, let atone the energy you have left for your personal life.

There is all the difference in the world between feeling stretched and challenged, where you are working in the 'flow', effectively and efficiently, and when you feel hurried, always stretching to catch up on out of control events. This introduces the notion of **stress**.

Stress is both a good thing and a bad thing - too little and we <u>Rust</u> <u>Out</u> too much and we <u>Burn</u> <u>Out</u>. So **stress** has a positive side as well as a negative one. The positive side is stimulus, such as responding

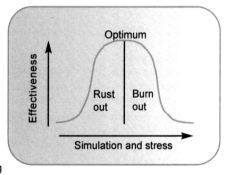

to challenges, with the buzz that can result. Another perspective is that the only time we won't ever encounter some **stress** is when we are dead!

The **Self Directing** approach to stress is through managing your own **stress** environment, which includes knowing what kind of **stress** is productive for you and what is not, and what works for you in terms of the way you handle it.

Knowing what works for you, whether it is meditation, physical activity and exercise, obtaining collaborative support from others, or whatever, is priceless on those occasions when we are overtaken.

Being **Self Directing** also means that you will take a deliberate conscious view of what you want if you encounter one of the phenomena of today's *macho stress culture*. Do you play or don't you play? Either decision will have consequences which you will need to face up to and resolve.

It is not intended here to deal with **stress** in a more complete way, largely because there are many other texts available which will cover it, but it is clearly a factor which has to be taken into account in **Managing Your Own Workload**. This is also more than just time management, Time management is to do with how efficiently you spend your time, and there are many structured ways of managing this, which work varyingly well for different people.

Managing Your Own Workload is a much wider view of you how manage your job, not just your time. It involves taking responsibility for managing yourself, what you can do, negotiating timescales, etc. It also requires us to be honest with ourselves about the kind of person we are (see chapter 6 - Understanding Yourself & Others) and in recognising where our problems lie and using Responsible Initiative to do something about them. We may, for example, be a person who likes to button things down very quickly - fine, but there may be useful information to come. Or we may prefer to keep everything very fluid until the deadline approaches - fine, but this tends to result in last minute panic.

Knowing how we tend to respond allows us to use our strengths and manage our weaknesses. Use the list on the following page to identify what is most likely to be holding you back.

The Common Time Wasters

Procrastination	Putting things off, particularly unpleasant tasks, or putting off making decisions even though they have been considered plenty of times.
Disorganisation	Not knowing where to find things, not being clear where to start and what to do, creating own chaos.
Not prioritising	Doing what comes to hand, or is pleasant and easy to do, rather than what is important or urgent.
Estimating time poorly	Not having an accurate time estimate of how long a task will take, including not allowing for interruptions, problems, etc.
Too willing to help others out	Being over-willing to help others at the expense of own work commitments.
Interruptions	Not managing to get into the 'flow' of work because of interruptions, necessary or not.
Not anticipating problems	Being taken by surprise by problems instead of anticipating them in advance.
Being impulsive	Acting when the whim takes you rather than on a more methodical basis.
Unable to say 'No'	Doing everything which comes your way, not being able to use positive negotiation to decide priorities, timescales, etc.
Losing track	Losing sense of what has to be done and by when in the flurry of activities.

Any more? What is your Achilles heel? What **Self Directing** action can you take to manage your own workload?

Chapter 6; Understanding Yourself & Others

Effective achievers are very perceptive about themselves. They deploy their strengths well and face up to their weaknesses, finding ways to manage them instead of just denying or ignoring them. The more competent people are, the more they are conscious of the diversity of other people - their strengths and corresponding weaknesses - and are able to recognise and work with their strengths. This is **Interdependence**, where the diversity and capacity of others is recognised and productively used.

There are many quotes to highlight the importance of **Understanding Yourself and Others**, in particular from Swiss psychologist, Dr Carl G Jung, on whose theories many psychometric tools are based.

'To understand others you first need to understand yourself' - Anon

'If one does not understand a person, one tends to regard him as a fool' - Dr Carl G Jung

'The less we have in common with a person the more likely we are to see their weaknesses instead of their strengths' - Dr Carl G Jung

'Every advance, every conceptual achievement of mankind, has been connected with an advance in self-awareness' - Dr Carl G Jung

'If we did all the things we were capable of doing, we would literally astound ourselves.' - Thomas Edison

There are some other powerful reasons for understanding yourself, and others, better. These include:

a) Giving you insight into what kind of work and work context suits you best, so you can be more successful and fulfilled.

b) As a basis for understanding and resolving difficulties with other people, including so called but inappropriately named 'personality clashes'.

c) Discovering perhaps dormant talents that you have, which have yet to be exploited and fulfilled.

d) As a basis for developing further the 'emotional competences' of dealing highly productively with other people, sometimes called interpersonal skills. These are particularly important for people who aspire to management. They are also important in proceeding beyond the baseline competence of expertise, and matter enormously in the way that expertise is deployed and used successfully.

Introduction to The Johari Window

In developing oneself and relationships with those around us it is important for us to both give and receive feedback. This must be done with an overall mindset of **Positive Regard** and **Genuineness** with the aim of enhancing the relationship and enabling yourself and others to grow. This is the **Self Directing** approach, leading to true **Interdependence**.

There are many models used for giving and receiving feedback, and we will look at some useful techniques in the next chapter. But one extremely helpful model was devised by American psychologists, Jo Lufts and Harry Ingham, in the 1950s while researching team working. It is aptly named The **Johari Window** which we will look at next.

The Johari Window

	Known to Self	Unknown to Self
Known to others	**Public**	**Blind**
Unknown to Others	**Private**	**Unknown**

The model is based on the premise that an individual will know themselves, to a greater or lesser extent, and that those around them - people with whom they work, their family and friends - will also know them by what and how they say and do things.

Public Pane: This concerns that area of oneself about which there are no secrets. I might know, for example, that I am a poor planner and get irritated by what I see as unnecessary detail when deciding on a course of action. Those around me will also know this because I might tell them, or they might observe it simply from my reactions in that type of situation.

Private Pane: This contains those bits of self-knowledge which I choose not to broadcast or reveal. Perhaps I feel nervous when making presentations, or alternatively find confronting discipline issues difficult.

Blind Pane: This pane is particularly significant. Contained in this part of the window are those behaviours which others see and experience when dealing with me, but about which I am ignorant or blind. For example, I might be totally unaware of how aggressive I appear when debating a work issue, or how my habit of looking at my watch during an appraisal interview gives the impression of impatience or indifference.

Unknown Pane: The final part of the window represents the unknown. That is, the behaviours or reactions I might have in a situation yet to be experienced. We all have ideas about how we would handle the masked raider, but until that situation arises, no-one will know, least of all me!

Those people who can best manage themselves and their environment, be it at work or socially, are those people who have consciously enlarged the first pane of their window. The Public, open side of themselves - what they know about themselves, their strengths and weaknesses, and also what those around them know and accept - is increased.

This widening of the Public pane of the Johari's Window Model is achieved through two clear behaviours - <u>DISCLOSURE</u> and <u>FEEDBACK</u>.

The *Private* pane can be reduced by the simple practice of being open with others. If I am unsure of my position in a particular meeting, I can say so. Or, if I am finding a colleague's approach frustrating at a particular time, I say so. This openness can also be seen as being **Genuine** with others; they are able to see exactly what is going on and can respond accordingly.

Perhaps the most valuable movement that can be made is the "drawing back of the curtains' on the Blind part of the window. This is done through the seeking of feedback from those around you and, very importantly, the skilled reception of that feedback from the potentially unskilled giver. Getting a clearer view of how others see us, and how our behaviour impacts on them, and then choosing how to use that information for our own development, is a very powerful skill indeed. It is often the case that we are unable to hear what people are really saying to us, but it is only when we do that we are able to test out the reality of who we are and are able to grow.

With regard to the *Unknown* pane, we are more rich and complex than we or others know. From time to time something will happen - maybe it is felt or heard or dreamed - and something from our unconscious is revealed to us. Then we know what we have never known before, and this knowledge too enables us to grow.

Chapter 7: Managing Your Own Learning & Development

'Give a man a fish and he has a meal - teach a man how to fish and he can eat for life.'

So it is with learning and development. Self Directing People have learned, so to speak, to fish for themselves, while Dependent People are more likely to expect the organisation to take charge of their training and development.

Self Directing People see the need to invest in their own business and success by taking an active approach to their own learning and continuous development. This is not just through taught courses, they use their everyday work environment to actively learn. Also, it is more than just through experience on the job, it is the way they make best use of that experience which really matters. They also do not rely just on enhancing their technical expertise, but on the way it is carried into effect. They use change as a learning opportunity.

In particular they …

- Understand how to actively learn as a process
- Establish for themselves what is required for success
- Seek and use feedback well
- Deal with mistakes productively

Learning & Change, Change & Learning

Change is another word for learning. Those who are already learning, continuously, are the people who can ride the waves of change. Change does not have to be forced on us by crisis or calamity, rather it is part of continuous learning. What it does require, however, is for each one of us to take charge of our own learning.

We all assume that we know how we learn. Often the assumption is based on being taught. Learning though is:
• a cycle of different activities
• a double loop process, which involves both solving the particular problem and developing the habit of learning
• best carried out in 'real life'
• a process of discovery, where we must each be our own discoverer
All this requires us, as individuals, to take Responsible Initiative for managing our own learning and development, for receiving and dealing with feedback well and proactively, for harnessing the realities of everyday work experience to learn and grow. Learning is a cycle in that it is like a wheel that is kept in motion by a series of jolts - the faster the wheel or cycle moves, the faster we learn. In this cycle there are four stages, each one of them important for real learning. The cycle and its stages is shown over the page.

When you look at the diagram, it seems very obvious ... it is. Most people, however, are more comfortable with, and thus tend to use more, particular stages of the cycle. Really effective learners though have well developed skills for each stage of the process, or know themselves sufficiently well to be aware of what they tend to neglect, and thus compensate for it - eg Reflection. Equally, some people can get stuck in one or other stage of the cycle, or take short cuts across it. Take a look and see what you think.

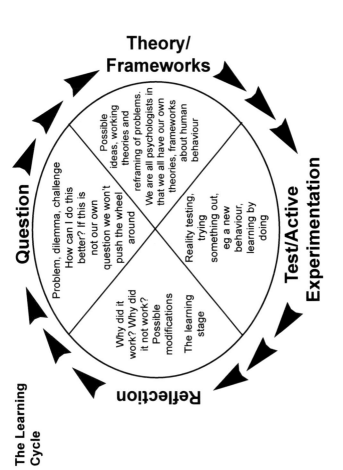

The Learning Cycle

Theory/Frameworks

Question

Test/Active Experimentation

Reflection

Possible ideas, working theories and reframing of problems. We are all psychologists in that we all have our own theories, frameworks about human behaviour

Problem, dilemma, challenge How can I do this better? If this is not our own question we won't push the wheel around

Reality testing, trying something out, eg a new behaviour, learning by doing

Why did it work? Why did it not work? Possible modifications

The learning stage

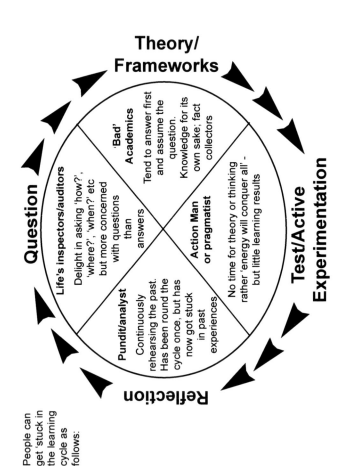

People can get 'stuck in the learning cycle as follows:

Theory/Frameworks

Question

Test/Active Experimentation

Reflection

'Bad' Academics

Tend to answer first and assume the question. Knowledge for its own sake; fact collectors

Life's inspectors/auditors

Delight in asking 'how?', 'where?', 'when?' etc but more concerned with questions than answers

Action Man or pragmatist

No time for theory or thinking rather 'energy will conquer all' - but little learning results

Pundit/analyst

Continuously rehearsing the past. Has been round the cycle once, but has now got stuck in past experiences

82

Necessary conditions for comfortable change and effective continuous learning:

Those who learn best, and change most comfortably...
• take responsibility for themselves and their future
• have a clear view of what they want that future to be
• want to make sure they can get it, and believe they can
• have an ability to see things, problems, situations in other ways - to 'reframe' them
• have a negative capability, so they can live with mistakes and failures without being downhearted or dismayed

They also avoid the things that can often block our way...
• the *'they'* syndrome
• fatality/humility
• the *theft* or *leaking* of their purpose
• a missing *forgiveness*

Adapted by Charles Handy

Dealing with Mistakes Productively

Many of us have been taught from an early age that mistakes are bad, Of course those mistakes to do with being slipshod, careless or irresponsible are, But unless we make mistakes we won't learn. If we are paralysed by the fear of making mistakes we won't try anything new. We become trapped in the comfort and security of the well tried and known, and are ill-equipped to deal with change.

Another way of looking at mistakes is to see them as something from which we can learn, and also that they are an inevitable part of exploration. Some companies become uneasy when their senior managers don't make any mistakes as this could be because they are not taking any risks or are unwilling to try out new initiatives.

What really matters is how mistakes are dealt with, and whether they are learned from or just repeated. **Self Directing Learners** are prepared to make 'genuine' mistakes, not deliberately but responsibly, as part of their learning, and when they do occur see them as **Positive Mistakes** from which they can learn and develop. This means taking **Personal Responsibility** for them and not blaming others, over-reacting or allowing their self-esteem to be damaged, but importantly mining them for learning. It also involves seeking and receiving feedback well.

Seeking & Receiving Feedback

Feedback, whether positive or negative, is invaluable. It helps us to be more effective and to learn and grow. Unfortunately, feedback or criticism is often given unskilfully and our natural defence mechanisms swing into action; this causes us to 'shoot the messenger' instead of really hearing the message.

This is likely to be because it is ingrained in most of us, from a very early age, that mistakes are bad. We have to wriggle out from under the mistake and maintain our innocence, using a range of well-worn approaches - eg 'It came off in my hand, mum!'

As a result, we make it exceptionally difficult and frustrating for the giver -who has had to steel themselves for the task in the first place - and who leaves the interview with all their beliefs confirmed, 'There's no point in talking to him - he's so dammed prickly!'

However, it is not just people's perceptions of us that are damaged by poor reception of feedback. We are cutting ourselves off from priceless data that we can use to really manage personal growth. There is also the danger that mistakes which we have made are not explored and learned from, and remain as tiger traps' for us to fall into, time and time again.

So, the first shift required is one of attitude ...

> *'Mistakes help me become more competent,*
> *so help me to see where I've made them.'*

Below are some techniques which should ease the process of receiving feedback however it is delivered, and will also ensure that you derive maximum benefit from the process.

• Appreciate the giver
If you recognise the difficulty the giver may be experiencing in delivering the message and appreciate their intent is to help, you will not only find it easier to suppress your 'defence mechanisms' but will also encourage the giver to give more. Make a point of thanking them for their feedback.

• Reflecting Back
Make sure you are really picking up the message by reflecting back what you have heard – *'I see what you mean, my lack of preparation must have been obvious to the client.'*

• Probing for Examples
If you are serious about using the feedback to make changes you need as much clarity as you can get. Probe the giver until you are sure you know what is meant – *'Im not sure I understand - can you give me an example of when I appeared unprepared?'*

• Taking Action
Show the giver that it has been worthwhile talking to you by telling them what you are going to do as a result of the feedback.

• Ask for Further Feedback
Demonstrate that you value what they have said; ask them for further feedback in the future on how you are performing in the area under discussion, or other related areas.

In some situations you may feel that you are not getting enough feedback to help you learn and develop. If this is the case, take the **Self Directing** approach of asking for it.

Feedback often involves both positive as well as negative feedback. Sometimes managers are relatively unskilled at giving positive feedback and use very generalised phrases such as 'I liked that', 'That was good', 'You performed well', etc. Although this may give you a warm glow and reassure you that you are going in the right direction, it is not as helpful as it might be. It is more valuable to your learning to know what aspects were liked and why, for example, in which case you need to probe more to understand what specifically is being valued.

Establish What is Required for Success

When you start a new job, project or task, or when you work with a new client for the first time, it pays to take **Responsible Initiative** to establish what the success criteria are. In this way you can direct and focus your efforts on the expectations required, and turn in a highly successful performance first time round. This is a highly proactive approach to learning as it gets the success criteria established at the outset.

The key technique to use is the **Critical Incident Interviewing** one, described in Chapter 3. One of the best ways of impressing your manager or a new client at the outset is to ask, not from the perspective of a **Dependent Subordinate**, but from that of a person using **Responsible Initiative**. The **Critical Incident** technique involves getting the other person to give particular examples of good or poor outcomes or behaviours, and is a powerful way of getting clarity on expectations.

Chapter 8: Managing Your Own Career

No-one is as interested in your career as you are. Not your manager (although he or she may be supportive), not the organisation, no-one! We are back to the point of you managing your own business (your career) in a Self Directing way. Otherwise you won't achieve what you want. This is of course supposing you know what you want. More, your career is part of your life overall, so your career needs to be seen in this context. So what we are talking about is both **Career** and **Life Planning** they are part and parcel of each other. **Self Directing Attitudes** and **Skills** make a crucial difference in life overall and not just in the workplace.

Firstly, it is useful to review what is your own business (your career) and in what business context your business is now being managed. Calculate what you expect to earn, including any fringe benefits, over your thirty to forty years of work. It is likely that you will find yourself as managing director of a million or multi-million pound business. If your success criteria include financial ones, there are obvious implications here. But the once in a lifetime opportunity to fulfil your goals, dreams and aspirations, wont happen by itself. A salutary way of thinking about this is to reflect on what your obituary will say about you - in just half a dozen words!

Careers now are being managed in a different business context from yesteryear, where career planning was managed by the organisation and career paths were visible and often promised. It may be that the job you will have in five years time doesn't currently exist. In short, the context has changed where instead of taking a **farming** approach (planting seeds in a patch of ground, nurturing them over time, etc) a more appropriate approach today is a **hunter gatherer** one, which involves looking for, and finding, the opportunities. This requires advanced preparation and having the skills to make best use of the opportunities through a **Self Directing** approach.

At the most basic level, most people's financial security comes from their ability to earn money. The first rule of warfare is said to be to protect your home base - in our terms to secure our capacity to earn a good living. This requires keeping our skills current and in tune with modern and evolving requirements. These are not just based on technical expertise, but on the emotional competence abilities to deliver them well. Above all, it means being **flexible**, in coping well with new ways of working and change. It used to be said, for example, that to be a 'Jack of all trades was to be a master of none'; today's requirements are more in the direction of being a Jack of all trades and a master of some.

To summarise then, at its lowest level security comes not from being employed, but from being **employable**, and it is in this that the concepts of taking responsibility for your own learning **and** for your own career join forces. But this is to see it at its lowest level, albeit a fundamentally important one. If our horizon is raised above this, there is much more to play for in terms of our own success, satisfaction and achievement. Is what we are experiencing at present 'as good as it gets' or could it be made to get better?

The first place to start, of course, is to get greater clarity on what you want, that is, what your own definition of success is. As the saying goes, 'if you don't know where you are going, any road will get you there'. This applies not just to your career, but your life overall - the two are intertwined.

A good number of us are caught up in the **SWAMP**, having some vague wishes of what we want to be doing some time away out into the future. It is all very general and way off. For example, we may want to retire early but are making no financial provision for this. Somehow we think it may happen by luck or by winning the lottery! Or we think that we may want to become a senior manager, but feel it will be OK to learn the skills required once we have been offered the post. We are reluctant to think through specifically what we want to do, now, as the first step towards our future aims or dreams.

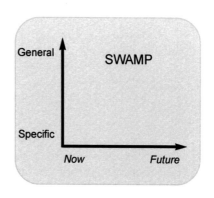

When in the **SWAMP** little is likely to happen, except by chance. Luck rarely meets opportunity because there has been no preparation, The successful, achieving people know where they want to be going, and start taking specific steps now to commence their journey. They also know that they have to be flexible and adaptable, because circumstances and wants may change around them in the future, but unless they get mobilised to march in the direction they want to go, nothing will happen anyway. So, they successfully combine **purpose** and **focus** with **adaptability** keeping their eyes open to the other opportunities and choices they discover en route.

All this focuses on 'success' and what it implies and means for **you** in both career and life terms. It was said earlier that no-one is as interested in your career as you are. There is an exception to this, and that is when you are living for other people's expectations - perhaps your parents, perhaps others? Getting clarity on your own definition of success is the first important step in achieving that success.

For example, to start this process, do you see this success being based on:

Advancement	Where you have greater responsibility, influence, status, etc, and correspondingly greater rewards. in many ways this is the traditional definition of success.
Context & Meaning	Working with an organisation which matches your values and attributes, and which provides a purpose and goals with which you can strongly identify.
Personal	Life style and having a good balance between home and work. Contributing in a wider society outside work.

...or on all three, but to a different proportion and emphasis for they are not mutually exclusive?

A very useful tool for identifying the kind of environment that you will find most appealing *at the present* time is the Motivation Inventory (by Dr Derek Biddle), available through Ali Stewart & Co. '*At the present time*' is stressed because needs do change over time. This inventory will also enable you to compare what you are getting from your present job with your defined needs in the areas of **People**, **Achievement** and **Enjoyment**. It may be that not all your needs are being met; if this is the case, then avoid moving automatically to 'the grass is greener' syndrome, but take a balanced view. You may be getting much of what you want, and the way ahead may be to achieve the missing part of being **Self Directing** and achieving it, either inside or outside work.

It has been highlighted that you are running your own business, but very few of us give thought or attention to preparing a business plan for our own business, although it is one of the first disciplines of running a business. This would be a very good exercise for you to do and there is a plan at the end of this chapter so you can make a start.

The world of work is now a very fluid one. The idea of earlier generations, when people would have a job for life is long gone. Loyalty just isn't enough. Job security and career management are what you make of it from your own resources, by taking a **Self Directing** approach to it, or not. But the other side of the coin is that the spectrum of opportunity is in many ways much larger than it was, that is for those people who have equipped themselves to make best use of it. The following priorities will help.

1 Have the mindset of Managing Your Own Business
Keep in mind that you are Managing Director of your own business - you - even when you are an employee of an organisation. This will help you stay proactive and **Self Directing** in **Managing Your Own Career**.

2 Invest in Your Own Business
Would you invest in a business that won't invest in itself? No,so invest in yourself by developing and enhancing your own skills, abilities and capacity to learn.

3 Maintain Visibility
Ensure that your good work and successes are noticed. Take opportunities to demonstrate that you can make a difference and add value.

4 Network Actively
Build your network of contacts, both within and outside your current organisation. Many career opportunities are generated this way and it is also a useful 'insurance' policy.

5 Scan the Market

Keep abreast of what is happening in the career market (internally and externally) and developments within it. Remember though to realistically appraise what you already have.

6. Keep 'Interviewee' Skills Current

The "moment of truth' in many career opportunities is the selection interview process. It is perhaps more difficult and nerve-wracking to do oneself justice if the process hasn't been experienced for some time. Some people even go as far as to make sure they experience a selection interview at least yearly to make sure their skills are still current and effective.

7 Manage Relationships Well

Remember, as a **Self Directing Professional**, you are managing your boss as well as the other way round, and the way you deal with co-workers will be key to your success. It has been stressed that Emotional Intelligence is now regarded as important in organisational life. Technical ability is no longer enough.

8. Prioritise and Balance Your Needs

It is a reality that it is rare indeed for anyone to have everything they want at the same time. **Self Directing People** realise this and manage their situation, prioritising and maximising certain wants while balancing others. When needs change, perhaps gradually, perhaps suddenly through a life changing event, they are able to re-evaluate and reach a new harmony about what is most important to them now.

9 Managing Change to Your Advantage

It is said that, like death and taxes, change is inevitable. And so it is, We may be able to deny it in our private lives - possibly to our detriment - but to put at risk the assets of our own business by doing so is certainly not smart. Necessary change - in skills, working practice, technology, etc - will happen. The choice is whether we can respond **flexibly** to it by using it, rather than letting it disable us, Key to this is to seek and identify the opportunities in such change.

10. Have a Fall-back Plan

Sometimes events occur, almost like a stray meteor, unforeseen and random. One such may be a job loss, through no fault of your own. It has happened to many people. It pays to have a **Plan B**, sufficiently thought through and ready. Otherwise, should such an event occur, it can cause you to make decisions when you are least able to do so - when you are perhaps experiencing the shock, stress and anger of what has happened. It is for this reason that people sometimes make inappropriate decisions about what to do next. Having a 'draft' **Plan B** in advance helps enormously in managing such a situation with clarity, direction - and even panache!

Typical Business Plan, *Career Plan* ... <u>and Your Own Plan</u>

Business Objectives *(3 - 5 year period)*
Career objectives - Objectives in terms of type of work, level, industry, location, experience sought
<u>My plan</u> -

Business History *Are the objectives realistic in terms of the business' history?*
Career progression - Patterns and achievements observable to date in your track record. Are the objectives realistic in terms of your career history?
<u>My plan</u> -

Background of the Management Team (You!)
Self - Your personal experience, responsibilities, and needs/plans for further development
<u>My plan</u> -

Market for the Business
Market for employment - Personal skills, qualifications, record of experience; compared with that required or expected in the market. The employment market.
<u>My plan</u> -

Products
Personal qualities and skills - What are the key aspects of your personality and skills, which could be valuable for an employer?
<u>My plan</u> -

Pricing Policy
Salary - What are your short and long term requirements? Are you prepared to accept lower earnings to acquire broad based experience?
<u>My plan</u> -

Suppliers
Employers & network - How do your current and potential employers stack up in terms of what they can offer you? How can your network help you?
<u>My plan</u> -

Capital Assets
Personal resources - What is your financial status? What are your commitments? Could you fund yourself through a full-time course of study? Do you have the discipline required to do evening study?
<u>My plan</u> -

Contingency Plans - (Plan B)
Contingency plans - What you will do if you fail to achieve your objectives, or lose your present job?
My plan -

Chapter 9: Postscript - Putting It All Together

There are people who succeed in life and work, who know what fulfilment and success means for them, and how to achieve this. There are others who don't, where life and luck are always thought to be conspiring against them, where the 'system' is wrong and 'they', that is other people, hold the keys to their fate.

The difference between these two situations is, first and foremost, a mindset which is to do with being **Self Directing**, or not and taking **Responsible Initiative** for their own learning and success. They manage their situation rather than being managed by it. They are not victims but glorious survivors.

Most people of course are neither of these extremes. Most in fact operate in the direction of being **Self Directing**. But, we are perhaps not as 'fit' at this as we might be. For all life's pressing reasons we often don't invest the relatively small amount of time and effort that makes the difference, not just for the work situation, but in terms of life overall. The payoff for this personal investment can be enormous, in wellbeing, competence and confidence, and in achieving whatever we want to achieve. This latter is of course the starting point for everyone's definition of personal success as unique and legitimate.

This guide gives the opportunity to review and enhance both our thinking and our skills. Both are necessary; our fate is determined by the view we take of life and work, but without certain skills applicable to both life generally as well as work, little will happen. These skills are generic, applicable to many situations, no matter what line of work or life you happen to be in. Again, most people have a good level of such skills already, the idea is to build on these.

There are seven of these skills of importance. **Questioning and Listening** excellently will enable you to get information you want and need in a manner which is both thorough and highly acceptable. Some techniques such as Refocusing and Probing are introduced. Then there is also **Negotiation and Influence** to enable you to get what you want while taking other people's needs - and negotiating styles - into account, and also to manage conflict. **Managing Your Own Workload** - instead of being managed by it - is another key skill, and one which not only reduces unnecessary stress and hassle, but positions you to achieve your commitments with grace, flow and success.

Understanding Your Own and Others' Strengths is a must in this age of Emotional Intelligence where, despite your technical specialism, how you bring the work into fruition and not just the task itself, provides the added value. Additionally knowing your strengths and weaknesses will allow you to make full effective use of the former and to manage the latter. Part of this is in understanding how you **Manage Your Own Learning and Development** - including taking personal responsibility for it - so that your skills and abilities not only stay current and valuable, but that you can stay *flexible* to meet new situations and opportunities.

You will have nous and a keen **Strategic Business Awareness**, able to see how what you are doing fits in with the bigger picture, problems are anticipated and opportunities spotted. You also pay attention to the tactical and operational aspects skilfully and well.

Finally, there is **Managing Your Own Career**, for no-one will care about this as much as you do. You are in effect managing your own business which may be part of a larger one at the present time. Like any business the starting point requires you to have a business plan, and to know the strengths, weaknesses, opportunities and threats of your own business. In all this the most important thing of all is to know what you want and what is the definition of success for you, so it can be achieved?

All these skills are of course **Interdependent** and mutually reinforce each other. They are the **Self Directing** skills for life.

NOTES

NOTES

NOTES

NOTES